# THE
# SOLAR SYSTEM

**ROYAL OBSERVATORY GREENWICH**

First published in 2021 by the National Maritime Museum, Park Row, Greenwich, London SE10 9NF

ISBN: 978-1-906367-78-7

The Royal Observatory in Greenwich, London, is the home of Greenwich Mean Time (GMT), the Prime Meridian of the world and London's only planetarium.

rmg.co.uk

Text © National Maritime Museum, London

All rights reserved. No part of this publication may be reproduced, stored in or introduced into a retrieval system, or transmitted in any form, or by any means (electronic, mechanical, photocopying, recording or otherwise) without the prior written permission of the publisher. Any person who commits any unauthorised act in relation to this publication may be liable to criminal prosecution and civil claims for damages.

A CIP catalogue record for this book is available from the British Library.

Designed by Matt Windsor at
The Design Garden

With special thanks to Dhara Patel

Printed and bound in Spain by Grafo

10 9 8 7 6 5 4 3 2 1

Images © National Maritime Museum, Greenwich, London except those listed below: p5 NASA, p6 NASA/JPL-Caltech, p7 NASA Goddard, p9 NASA/JPL-Caltech, p10 NASA/SDO, AIA, p12 Nerthuz/Shutterstock.com, p14 Marcel Clemens/Shutterstock.com, p15 NASA/JPL, p16 NASA, p17 Jamen Percy/Shutterstock.com, p18 NASA/Goddard Space Flight Center/Arizona State University, p19 NASA, p20 NASA/USGS, p21 NASA/JPL/USGS, p21 NASA/JPL-Caltech, p22 Marcel Clemens/Shutterstock.com, p23 Tristan3D/Shutterstock.com, p24 NASA/JPL, p25 NASA, p25 NASA/JPL-Caltech/Space Science Institute, p26 Marcel Clemens/Shutterstock.com, p28 Marcel Clemens/Shutterstock.com, p29 NASA/JPL, p29 NASA/JPL/Universities Space Research Association/Lunar & Planetary Institute, p33 NASA/Johns Hopkins University Applied Physics Laboratory/Southwest Research Institute, p34, NASA/JPL-Caltech/UCLA/MPS/DLR/IDA (Ceres), Aleksandr Morrisovich/Shutterstock.com (Eris), Sudakarn Vivatvanichkul/Shutterstock.com (Haumea), Diego Barucco/Shutterstock.com (Makemake), p36 NASA/JPL/JHUAPL, p37 NASA/Bill Dunford (meteor), USGS National Map Data Download and Visualization Services (meteor crater), 38 NASA/Bill Dunford, p39 NASA/MSFC/Aaron Kingery, p40, Wikicommons (Maunder), MicroOne/Shutterstock.com (Huggins), p41 Wikicommons (Ahmad), Wikicommons (Herschel), NASA, ESA (Hubble), Wikicommons (Rubin), p42 Flickr commons (Payne-Gaposchkin), NASA (Burnell), p43 Mike Peel; Jodrell Bank Centre for Astrophysics, University of Manchester (Lovell), Flickr Commons (Clerke), p45 ESA/Herschel/PACS/L. Decin et al.Rigel (Betelgeuse),NASA/STScI Digitized Sky Survey/Noel Carboni (Rigel), NASA/JPL-Caltech/STScI (Orion Nebula), ESA/Hubble & NASA, G. Piotto (stars), p46 Péter Feltóti (Andromeda), p47 NASA, ESA, S. Beckwith (STScI) and the Hubble Heritage Team (STScI/AURA) (Whirlpool Galaxy), NASA/CXC/JPL-Caltech/STScI (Small Magellanic Cloud). Planets and astronaut illustrations throughout designed by Freepik.com

# THE SOLAR SYSTEM

## A Cosmic Adventure

### ELIZABETH AVERY

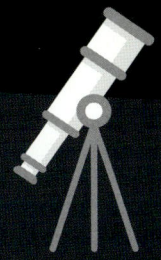

# Welcome to the Solar System!

The Solar System is a weird but wonderful place. Where else could you find sparkly rings, hexagonal storms and moons that look like giant potatoes?

Are you ready to find out more?
Read on, explorer!

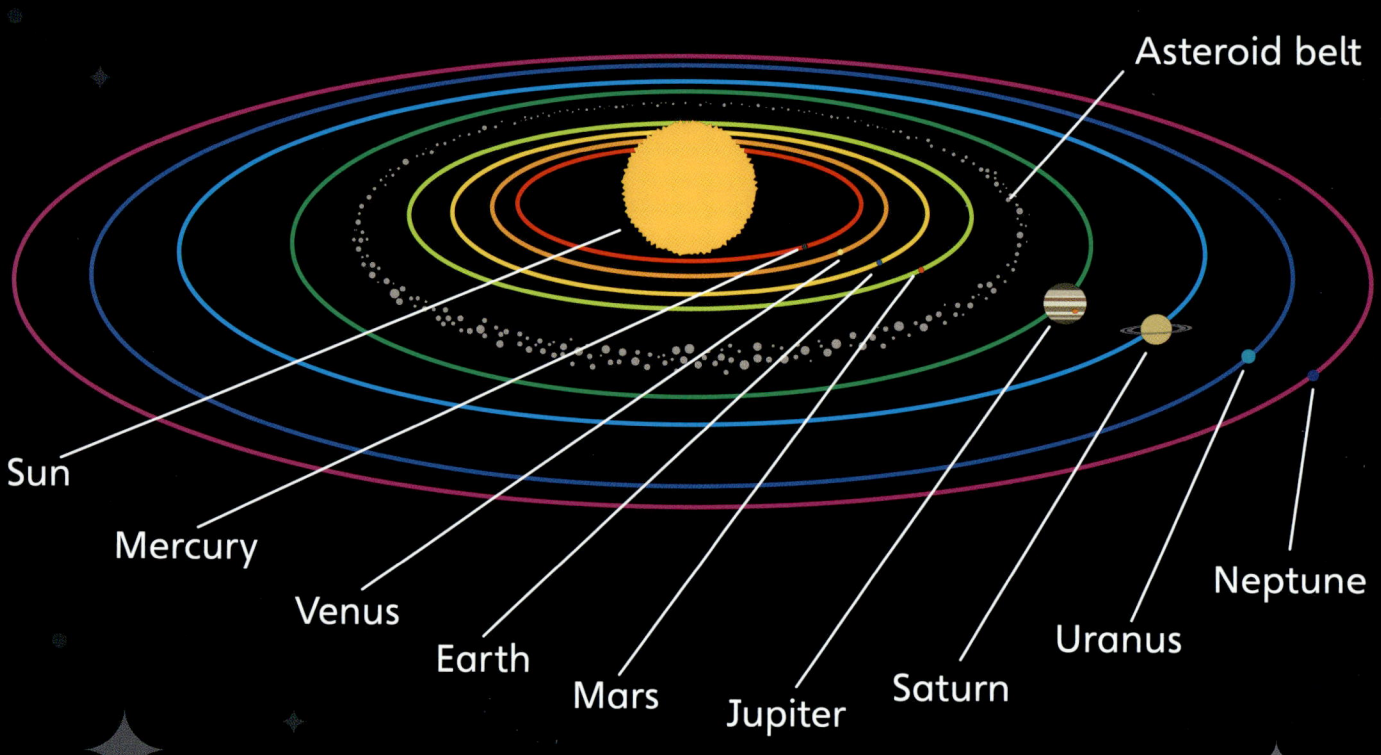

Asteroid belt
Sun
Mercury
Venus
Earth
Mars
Jupiter
Saturn
Uranus
Neptune

The *Apollo 11* mission launch, 1969

# Where are we?

Unless you are an alien lifeform from another planet (and some grown-ups can make you wonder) then you live on planet Earth. Earth is one of the eight planets within the Solar System, which also contains lots of space rocks and the Sun. The Solar System lives inside one of the arms of our spiral galaxy, the Milky Way.

The Milky Way

The Universe

Our galaxy has over 100 billion stars in it and lives in the Universe with over a billion other galaxies. Mind-meltingly brilliant, right?

Q+A: Is there anyone out there?
So far Earth is the only planet where life has been found. However, with so many galaxies out there with their own stars and planets, the chances of there being somewhere else that life could exist are pretty good, don't you think?

So where did our solar system come from? It started with a huge spinning cloud of gas and dust around 4.5 billion years ago – all sounds quite simple, doesn't it?

Scientists think an exploding star nearby may have given the cloud a little space nudge which caused it to start collapsing in on itself. As the cloud collapsed, it began to spin faster and faster and flatten out into a disc shape. The centre of the cloud then became very dense (this just means there was a lot of stuff in there). The result of all that spinning was something that looked a little like two fried eggs stuck back-to-back – not exactly the Solar System we know and love just yet. The centre of the disc got so roasting-toasting hot that it began to make its own light, and the Sun was born.

That was just the beginning though. There was still a huge spinning disc of gas and dust around our baby Sun. Over time, the disc began to cool and, thanks to magnetism and gravity, came together to form large, chunky space rocks.

These chunks started to smash together and got bigger and bigger – some were so big they became planets! Not all of them did, however, and there are still lots of smaller space rocks hurtling through space.

**FACT**
Our closest galactic neighbour is the Andromeda galaxy. But if you sent a text to someone living there, it would still take 2.5 million years to arrive!

**DID YOU KNOW?**
Distance in space is measured in light years. A light year is the distance that light (which travels faster than anything else we know of) can travel in one Earth year. That is 9,460,528,400,000 km! That's the equivalent of over 224 billion marathons!

**WOW!** At the centre of our galaxy is a supermassive black hole, which is a bit like an enormous space vacuum cleaner. It's so powerful it sucks everything in, even light! Black holes are tricksters though, because we can't actually see them but we know exactly what they're up to!

**Q+A: What are sunspots?**
Some parts of the Sun are cooler than others. The cool patches look darker and are called sunspots. Sometimes magnetic field lines get in a right twizzle near sunspots and get tangled up like a bowl of spaghetti. This can cause energy to explode from the Sun in solar flares.

# The Sun

Let's start with the brightest star in our solar system – well, the only one – the Sun! Do you know what makes the Sun so special? It is OURS, and without it we couldn't survive!

The Sun is a bit like a ringmaster in a circus and it really does call the shots. It contains 99.8% of all the material in the Solar System – yikes! The Sun keeps all of the Solar System's planets in check as they travel around it on their own paths; we call these space paths orbits. For us living on Earth, the Sun also affects day and night, seasons and weather conditions, as well as giving us spectacular light shows like the aurora.

The Sun is different to everything else in the Solar System because it gives out its own light. Planets, dwarf planets, moons and space rocks just reflect the Sun's light rather than making their own. The Sun's core, where it makes its light, is a scorching 15 million degrees Celsius, which is over 31,900 times hotter than the hottest planet, Venus – OUCH!

One day, the Sun will run out of fuel and it will puff up like a space puffer-fish and become a red giant, swelling so big that it will gobble up Mercury and Venus and maybe even Earth. After it has puffed away its outer layers all that will eventually be left is a white dwarf star. The Sun won't live forever but DON'T panic. None of this is predicted to happen for another five billion years.

**WOW!** The Sun is 109.2 times larger than Earth. If the Earth was the same size as a queen bumblebee the Sun would be the same size as a large brown bear.

**FACT**
It might look like an enormous ball of fire and lava but the Sun is actually a huge burning ball of superheated gas, known as plasma.

**REMEMBER!** Never look directly at the Sun as it can damage your eyes. If you want to check it out you can view it safely through a solar telescope which has a special shield, or through a pin-hole camera.

**FACT**

Mercury is named after the Roman god of messages and communication. In mythology Mercury the messenger travelled very quickly thanks to help from a winged helmet and shoe combination — sounds fancy, right? Because Mercury the planet is also super speedy the Romans thought it seemed like a good fit.

# Mercury

The first planet we reach on our adventure is the dinkiest in the Solar System – Mercury!

The temperature changes on Mercury are pretty bananas. In the daytime it can get to a super toasty 430°C – so hot that your body would effectively mummify. At night it can get to a seriously chilly -180°C, so cold that the tears on the surface of your eyes would evaporate and leave behind ice crystals – YIKES! Mercury has these wild temperature shifts because it doesn't have an atmosphere like Earth's. Instead, it has what we call an exosphere. Mercury warms up during the daytime, when the Sun is shining, but at night this heat escapes into the depths of space because the exosphere is too thin to hold on to it.

You may have heard the term 'exo' before; it means 'outside' in ancient Greek. A lobster has an EXOskeleton; they have a hard shell on the outside with all the squishy stuff protected underneath.

If we could protect ourselves from the deadly scorching and freezing conditions and actually visit Mercury, what would it be like? Well, a day would be as long as 176 Earth days. However, Mercury has a much shorter trip around the Sun than the other planets, so a year on Mercury is only 88 Earth days long! This all sounds very bonkers but because Mercury spins on its axis pretty slowly, it has long days, but because it whizzes around the Sun really quickly, it has short years.

**DID YOU KNOW?** Mercury is tiny compared to all the other planets! You could fit 16 Mercurys inside the Earth.

**WOW!** Mercury is a real little speed racer, travelling at 170,000 km per hour. That's 352 times faster than the fastest car on Earth!

**Q+A:** How far away from the Sun is Mercury? Mercury is 58 million km from the Sun. Although it is the closest planet to the Sun in our solar system it still takes 3.2 minutes for light from the Sun to reach Mercury!

### DID YOU KNOW?
Venus spins so slowly that you could take a leisurely cycle around the planet and always be able to see the Sun – it would never appear to set (if you could see it through the thick atmosphere!)

### DID YOU KNOW?
Because Venus is only tilted on its axis ever so slightly it doesn't have seasons!

# Venus

Next up we have Venus. Venus is over 108 million km away from the Sun. You would need to travel to the Moon and back 140 times to cover the same distance! It may be further away from the Sun than Mercury but it is actually hotter. In fact, it's the hottest planet in the Solar System. Temperatures on Venus can reach a whopping 470°C! That's so hot that you could cook a pizza on its surface without a pizza oven!

Venus is a funky little mover and actually spins on its axis the opposite way to the other planets — we call this 'retrograde motion'. Venus spins at a pretty chilled-out pace too, and takes 243 Earth days to make a whole spin on its axis. That is a little longer than a Venusian year — 225 days.

If you stood on the surface of Venus you would not last long at all. Not only would the pressure of the thick atmosphere squash you but you would also sizzle in the heat before choking on the poisonous gas — YIKES! Maybe not a great place for a holiday then…

Even if we could stand on the surface, we wouldn't see much! Spacecraft that have landed there and taken pictures show clouds that are so thick it is impossible to see through them. The atmosphere is a very interesting place to poke around — scientists have been getting very excited about what might be in there. It's filled with carbon dioxide, clouds of sulphuric acid and scientists have even observed lightning in there too!

**WOW!** There's a mountain on Venus called Maxwell Montes which is 11 km high — that's as tall as 2,000 giraffes!

**Q+A: Are there volcanoes on Venus?** Oh yes! There are more volcanoes on Venus than on any other planet in our solar system.

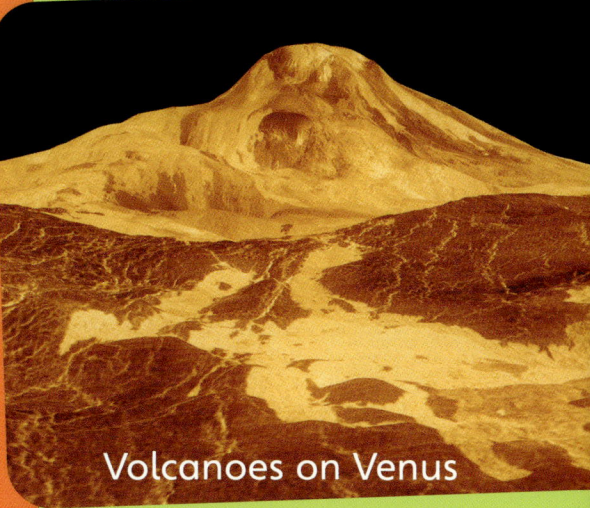

Volcanoes on Venus

**Q+A: Why is the sky blue?** When light from the Sun hits our atmosphere, it interacts with the molecules in it such as oxygen and nitrogen. These molecules scatter the light, which means they won't let it pass through in the lovely straight line it wants to travel in. Instead the light is deflected in all different directions and split up to look like a rainbow. The blue bit is scattered the most by the atmosphere and our eyes are beautifully sensitive to it, so this is what we see!

# Earth

Planet Earth is a pretty perfect place for us human beings to live. Earth is an ideal distance from the Sun, so it's not too hot, not too cold. It's just right; real Goldilocks conditions. No seriously, this region really is called the Goldilocks Zone. No, it's not filled with porridge-eating, bed-stealing bears! It's called this because it's in a region in space where water is liquid because the temperature is just right. This is important because water is one of the key things needed to support life.

Every so often the Sun spits large amounts of material into space – sort of like a space sneeze! We call this space sneeze the 'solar wind'. This could be very dangerous for us on Earth, however, we have a super-amazing invisible defence system – our own magnetic force field as well as an atmosphere. The solar wind high energy particles get caught up in the Earth's magnetic field lines which meet up at the north and south poles. It is here where they are able to break into our atmosphere – sneaky! When they do, they bump into and excite some of the atoms like nitrogen, oxygen and argon. These atoms don't like getting excited and having too much energy so will try and get rid of it in the form of colourful light. This works out really well for us because we are treated to a natural light display called *Aurora Borealis*, or the Northern Lights – thanks, particles!

*Aurora Borealis*

We hear about the Northern Lights a lot but did you know there are also Southern Lights? This is because the solar wind high energy particles can sneak into the atmosphere at the north AND south poles! The Northern Lights are called the *Aurora Borealis* and the Southern Lights are called the *Aurora Australis*.

**WOW!** The Earth has a circumference of 40,070 km. If the world's fastest cheetah ran non-stop at top speed it would take 15 days for it to get around the whole world! That would be one tired kitty!

**Q+A: We have seasons on Earth, do all planets?** Earth has seasons because it is tilted on its axis, but not all of the planets are tilted, so they don't have seasons.

**Q+A: How fast does the Moon move?** The Moon travels around the Earth in 27.3 days. To do a full cycle of all the lunar phases takes a little longer, at 29.5 days.

**WOW!** The Moon is covered with craters, which are big holes where space rocks have smashed into it over the years. Tycho crater is particularly impressive, being 85 km wide – that is bigger than the whole of London!

# The Moon

An astronaut's footprint on the Moon, taken on the *Apollo 11* mission in 1969

The Moon has been a constant source of interest for us on Earth. It is our closest neighbour and very own natural satellite. It is 3.7 times smaller than Earth, so if the Moon was the size of a Brussels sprout, the Earth would be the size of a grapefruit. The Moon is only 384,400 km away from us – although that's still a very long way! The largest giant squid ever recorded was almost 18 m long (eww) and you would need over 21.4 million of them lined up to reach the distance to the Moon. That would be one brilliant conga line though!

Yuri Gagarin may have been the first human in space in 1961 but we had to wait a few more years until anyone actually stepped foot on the Moon. On 20 July 1969 Neil Armstrong, Edwin Eugene Aldrin Jr. ('Buzz') and Michael Collins, as part of the *Apollo 11* crew, landed the Eagle lunar module on the Moon's surface. That's where the famous phrase 'The Eagle has landed' comes from!

So, the big question – could we live there? Well, the Moon has no air to breathe and the temperature swings between 127°C in the sunlight to -173°C out of the Sun – brrrrrrrrrr. We would have to take everything we needed with us right down to the air we breathe, but, in theory, humans could live there.

**FACT**
Although it looks like a light source, the Moon actually just reflects light from our Sun.

**Q+A: Is there a dark side of the Moon?** No, just a side of the Moon we do not see from Earth. The Moon and Earth are tidally locked. This means that the time it takes for the Moon to spin on its axis and travel around the Earth are the same so we always see the same side of the Moon facing us.

**DID YOU KNOW?** There are eight phases of the Moon. As the Moon moves around the Earth we see different amounts of the light reflected from the Moon's surface, so it appears to take on different shapes.

**Q+A: Does Mars have moons?** You bet it does! There are two small moons in orbit around Mars called Deimos and Phobos. Even though their names mean 'terror' and 'fear' they don't look very scary at all – in fact, they look more like giant space potatoes!

**WOW!** Sunsets on Mars look blue. That's right, blue! Why? Great question! Dust and molecules in the atmosphere of Mars mean that light from the Sun is scattered. It ends up being the blue part of this deflected light that we see.

# Mars

Mars might look like a hot and sizzly place, but don't let its red colour fool you – it is actually very cold! Mars is further away from the Sun than Earth so it does not get as much of the Sun's energy as we do. However, it does have four seasons during its year, just like the Earth. At the height of summer it can be 30°C (just like a warm summer's day in the UK) but in winter it can be below -140°C – three times colder than Antarctica! The seasons on Mars last around twice as long as they do on Earth – wow, imagine having summer holidays that long!

If there was a prize for the planet with the largest volcano it would go to… Mars! There is an extinct volcano on Mars called Olympus Mons that is so huge it would span the distance of over 20,000 blue whales.

Have you ever left your bike or scooter out in the rain? It's a risky business because it could rust! Mars looks VERY rusty because the iron in its rocks reacts with oxygen in the atmosphere to create rusty dust. This then gets flung around, making the planet look red from a distance.

A seriously amazing fact about Mars is if you were to jump around you would experience over 60% less gravity than on Earth. That means you would be able to jump a LOT higher. Imagine the bonkers world records being set at the Mars Olympics!

The volcano Olympus Mons

**FACT**

Mars is named after the Roman god of war. The Romans chose the name because its reddish colour reminded them of blood – gruesome!

The *Curiosity* rover

**Q+A: Has anyone found life on Mars?** No, not yet. Mars is an interesting place though and scientists are finding out new things all the time with the use of rovers, which are robots that they have sent to the planet to nose around. Keep your fingers crossed!

**DID YOU KNOW?** If Earth was the size of a cherry then Jupiter would be the size of a watermelon! That means it's large enough to fit more than 1,000 Earths inside it.

**WOW!** Days and nights on Jupiter are very short. It is light for only five hours each day and dark for around five hours too. That is less than half the normal day and night we have on Earth!

# Jupiter

Jupiter is the largest planet in the Solar System. It is called a gas giant because it's made of gas and, you guessed it, it's giant! If you tried to walk on its surface you would sink through. Scientists think it might have a solid core, and if it does it would be around the size of planet Earth.

It might look serene with its swirling, swooshing clouds but this is one seriously stormy planet. Jupiter hosts the largest storms in the Solar System. The biggest of all is called the Great Red Spot, a storm almost 1.3 times the size of the whole Earth. It is likely that Jupiter was the first planet to form so it makes sense that it was able to grow so big and mighty. It might actually have taken some of the material that should have gone into forming Mars too (how cheeky) which may explain why Mars is a little smaller than it should be. Greedy Jupiter!

Jupiter is a real dazzler with multi-coloured stripes going all the way around it. These bands are actually clouds that wrap around the whole planet. The different colours come from lots of different gases all swishing around together.

Jupiter has a bucket-load of moons! Scientists know of 79 different ones at the moment but astronomers just keep finding more all the time. In 1610, Galileo Galilei was the first person to observe moons travelling around Jupiter. We now call these moons the Galilean moons and they have the best names: Io, Europa, Ganymede and Callisto.

**The Galilean moons of Jupiter all have a little something special about them:**

### Io

The most volcanically active place in the Solar System.

### Ganymede

A real heavyweight moon; it's the largest moon in the Solar System.

### Callisto

The most battered moon in the Solar System and has a LOT of craters.

### Europa
A prime target to search for life. Scientists have found sodium chloride (table salt) and a liquid-water ocean. All we need is to find some fish and chips too and we would have ourselves a tasty moon dinner!

**WOW!** It rains on Titan, one of Saturn's moons, although the rain droplets are larger and slower than on Earth because of the thick atmosphere and lower gravity. They are made of liquid methane and more like the size of mini marshmallows.

**Q+A: Are there any other interesting moons?** Oh yes. We can't forget Enceladus. It shoots icy blasts of its ocean out into space – bonkers! This is very helpful because it has meant that scientists can sample the ocean to find out what it is made of. Thanks, Enceladus!

# Saturn

There's no question about it, Saturn is an interesting planet for sure. Like Jupiter, it's a gas giant, which means it's both humongous and made of gas with no solid surface. The funny thing about Saturn is that it is less dense than water so if you found a bath tub big enough it would float like a rubber duck!

Saturn is famous for its amazing rings that look like a giant diamond hula hoop. They are actually made up of ice and rock but you could be mistaken for thinking they are enormous gemstones! These ice and rock chunks can be as small as a flea or as big as a house!

Saturn has a LOT of moons, with over 80 known about at the moment. Some of Saturn's moons, such as Prometheus and Pandora, are known as shepherd moons. These play a particularly important role. Due to their gravitational effect, they keep the rings in the circular shape we see, a bit like a shepherd controls a flock of sheep. Clever, eh? Saturn's largest moon Titan is a real beast of a moon, and is actually bigger than the planet Mercury. The only moon larger than it in our solar system is Ganymede, but only by a smidge.

Ice and rock in Saturn's rings

**DID YOU KNOW?** When astronomer John Flamsteed was observing Saturn in the 17th century he didn't realise Saturn had rings. From his perspective they looked like handles!

**WOW!** Saturn also has some pretty bananas storms. Some of them are hexagonal, but no one knows why. It's a total mystery!

A hexagonal storm on Saturn

**DID YOU KNOW?** Uranus has a ring system! Oh yes, it actually has a few sets of rings. The inner-most set are dark grey but the ones further out are reddish and then blue – snazzy!

**Q+A: Does Uranus have moons?** Yes! The moons of Uranus are named after characters written by William Shakespeare and Alexander Pope, like Puck, Cordelia, Oberon, Ariel and Umbriel.

# Uranus

If you like cold winter days with thick, cosy socks and mugs of hot chocolate, then Uranus might be the planet for you. The coldest inhabited place on Earth, Oymyakon, in Russia, gets to a chilly -67.8°C, but Uranus, the coldest planet in our whole solar system, gets to -224°C!

Uranus dances a jazzy path through space. It travels around on its side! Scientists think it may have been knocked over by a very large space object early on in its life and has kept moving sideways ever since. Uranus's atmosphere is mainly made of hydrogen and helium with a little bit of methane. You may have heard of methane because it is an odourless gas that cows give off. An atmosphere made of cow farts?! Yuck!

Scientists discovered that different elements eat different bits of a light spectrum. This means they can work out what element they are looking at by studying the light spectrum. They found hydrogen sulphide on Uranus. Have you heard of it? It's a corrosive, poisonous and super-stinky gas that smells like rotten eggs – poor planet Uranus! Don't worry though, the smell would be the last thing on your mind if you visited – the freezing temperatures and lack of air to breathe would be a much bigger problem!

Absorption spectrum of mercury

Absorption spectrum of lithium

The absorption spectrum for mercury and lithium. The black lines show where each elements gobble up the light to make a unique signature spectrum.

**WOW!** How big is Uranus? Pretty big, it could fit 63 Earths inside it!

**FACT**

William Herschel discovered Uranus in 1781. It was the first planet to be found using a telescope as all of the closer planets can be seen with just your eyes!

**Q+A: How long are years and days on Uranus?** A year on Uranus is much longer than one on Earth, although a day is quite short! One year on Uranus is roughly equal to 84 Earth years! This means that seasons on Uranus last for 21 Earth years.

27

**FACT**

Triton spins the opposite way to other moons! Triton is the only moon in the Solar System that moves around its planet in the opposite direction to the way the planet rotates.

**WOW!** Scientists have discovered geysers on Triton that spew icy material 8 km into space! That's the same distance as 667 double-decker buses placed end-to-end. Yikes!

# Neptune

The last planet on our tour of the Solar System is Neptune, a gas giant and the most distant planet from the Sun. Some of the other planets have pretty wild winds but Neptune would win the medal for fastest winds in the Solar System. It also has a brilliantly named cloud pattern – Scooter! It makes it sound like a fun place to be, but it most definitely isn't!

If you like birthday cake (and who doesn't, right?) then sadly Neptune would not be the best place for you. It takes Neptune such a long time to go around the Sun that you would have to wait 165 Earth years between birthdays for your next cake – no thanks!

In ancient Roman mythology Neptune was the god of the seas. The planet doesn't actually have very much to do with the sea though, strangely, other than that it's blue. The blue colour actually comes from methane – just like with Uranus.

Neptune's discovery was a very curious business because it can't actually be seen with the naked eye. How did anyone find it then you ask? Good question, astronomer! With the wonderful world of maths, that's how! Astronomers knew there must be something else out there because Uranus's orbit was being affected but they couldn't see what was causing it. They suspected it might be a planet, and used snazzy maths to predict where this mystery planet might be. They went looking for it and they found Neptune!

The crescent shapes of Neptune and its moon Triton

**Q+A: Does Neptune have any moons?**
Oh yes! Neptune has 14 moons orbiting it, Triton being the biggest.

**DID YOU KNOW?**
The surface of Triton (one of Neptune's moons) looks like the skin of a cantaloupe melon! Size-wise there's a bit of a difference though, as the diameter of Triton is the equivalent width of 22.5 million large cantaloupe melons! That's a lot of fruit!

The rugged terrain of Triton's surface

# Did You Know?

The Sun is 150 million km from Earth. You would need to travel around the world 3,743 times to cover that distance!

If you look at the Moon just with your eyes you will see patches. The light bits are called highlands and the dark *maria* (Latin for 'seas'). These would have been filled with lava billions of years ago – imagine that!

Mars is a terrestrial planet. The word terrestrial comes from the Latin for Earth, *Terra*. The terrestrial planets are all Earth-like in that they have a solid surface made of mainly minerals or metals. Mercury, Venus, Earth and Mars are all terrestrial planets.

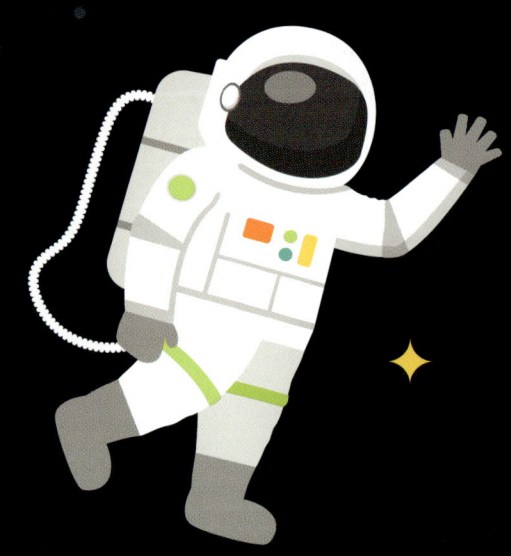

Venus is named after the Roman goddess of love – awwwww.

Saturn is the second largest planet in the Solar System and can fit more than 750 Earths inside it.

The Romans also named Jupiter after the king of the Roman gods. We refer to the gas giant planets Jupiter, Saturn, Uranus and Neptune as the Jovian planets, which just means they are associated with the monster planet Jupiter.

Uranus is the only planet to be named after a Greek god rather than a Roman one. It's named after Ouranos, the Greek god of the sky.

Neptune is roughly four times bigger than Earth. If Earth was the size of a tennis ball Neptune would be the size of a basketball!

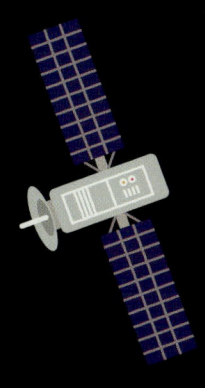

# What Else is Out There?

You may be wondering what's next? If Neptune is the last planet in our solar system surely there can't be anything else interesting left... can there? OH YES, there can!

## The Kuiper Belt

The Kuiper Belt is a region of space made of leftovers, which sounds a little odd, right? It's true, it's made up of leftover bits and bobs from when the Solar System formed. Astronomers think that if Neptune hadn't been there the leftovers could have come together to form something bigger like a planet. Neptune and its gravity put a stop to that though and instead left us with what we see today — a big, thick, doughnut-shaped region of space filled with icy space chunks!

The Kuiper Belt

# Pluto

We can also find Pluto in the Kuiper Belt. Did you know that Pluto used to be a planet? In 2006 the International Astronomical Union decided to rethink what could and couldn't be called a planet. They decided planets must:

- Be roughly spherical
☑ Pluto is shaped like a ball

- Go around the Sun
☑ Pluto does that too

- Clear its orbit (meaning the planet needs to clear its neighbourhood of nearby objects)
☒ Oh dear. Pluto has never cleared up its orbit. Well, two out of three was pretty good! However, this meant it was renamed a **dwarf planet** instead.

## HOW SMALL IS PLUTO?

**Pluto**
2,376 km wide

**The Moon**
3,474 km wide

**Earth**
12,742 km wide

# What other dwarf planets are there?

**Ceres.** This one sits within the asteroid belt and is the only dwarf planet to be found in the inner Solar System. It was actually classified as an asteroid for a long time until astronomers realised it qualified as a dwarf planet!

**Eris.** This dwarf planet can be found in the Kuiper Belt and is roughly the same size as Pluto. It is further away though, and light from the Sun takes more than nine hours to reach Eris.

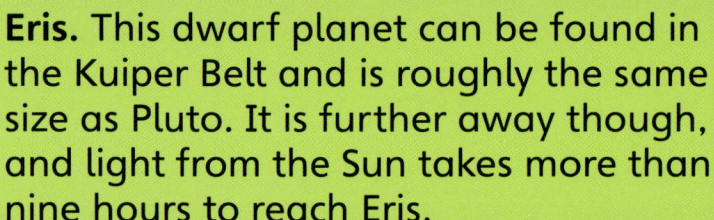

**Haumea.** Another Kuiper Belt resident. This dwarf planet rotates VERY fast. So fast, in fact, that it has warped into more of a rugby-ball shape!

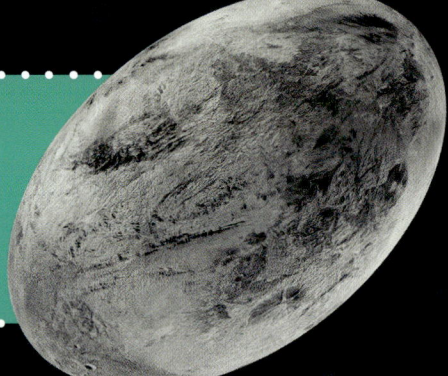

**Makemake.** This is also found in the Kuiper Belt. It is an important space object because, along with Eris, it was one of the main reasons astronomers decided they needed to reconsider the definitions of planets and dwarf planets.

# The Oort Cloud

Now we come to possibly one of the best-named bits of the Solar System – the Oort cloud. This region is sort of like a giant bubble which our whole solar system sits inside. The Oort cloud is believed to be made of mountain-sized pieces of space leftovers. Astronomers think there could be trillions of huge ice-mountains whizzing around out there – yikes!

Both the Kuiper Belt and Oort cloud contain comets. Scientists think that short-period comets (those that take less than 200 years to go around the Sun) come from the Kuiper Belt, and long-period comets (which take more than 200 years) come from the Oort cloud. 200 years doesn't sound very 'short' though, does it?!

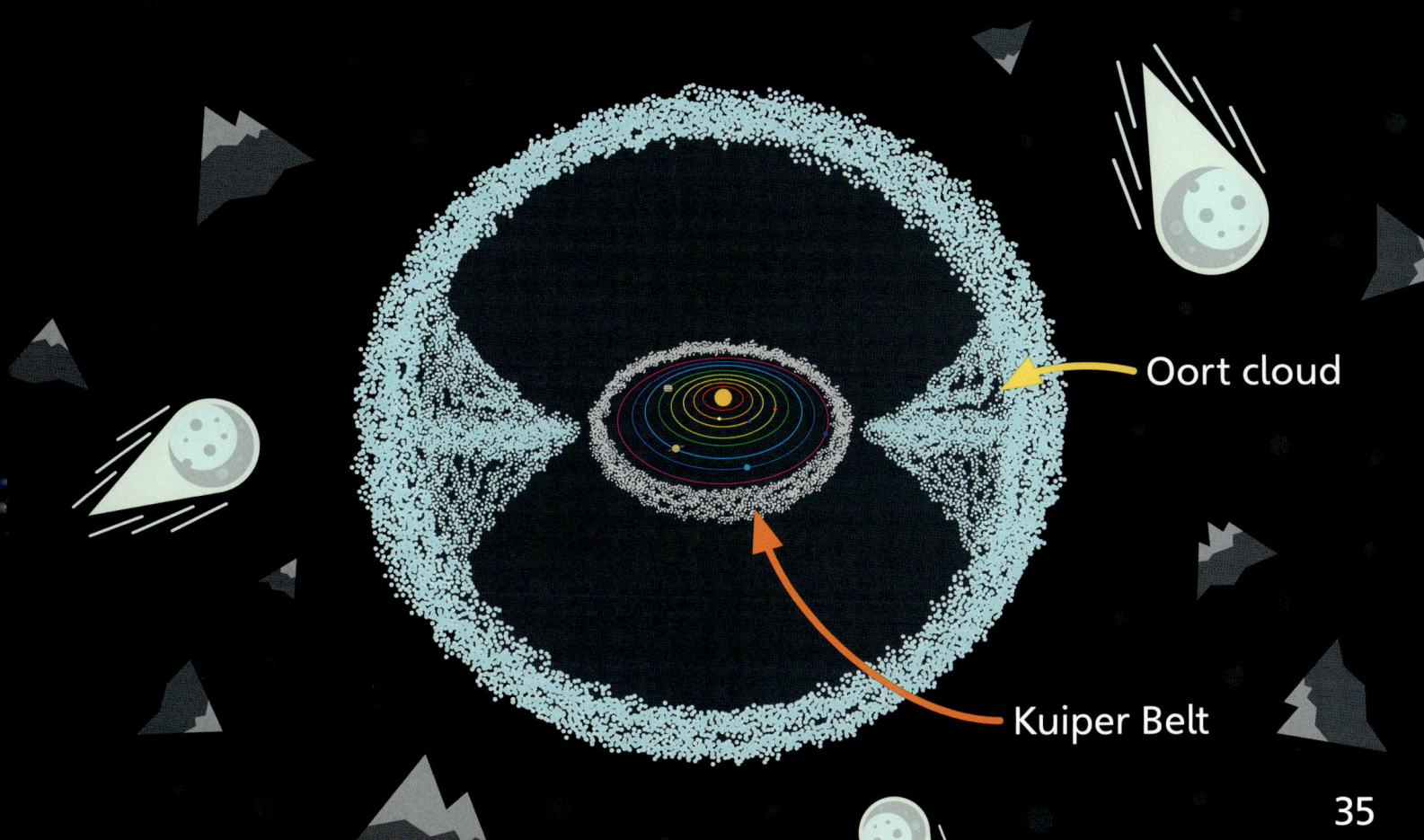

Oort cloud

Kuiper Belt

# Space Rocks!

There are all sorts of space rocks whizzing around in space alongside the planets and stars, including asteroids, meteoroids, meteors, meteorites and comets – let's find out the difference!

## Asteroids

Asteroids are space rocks that orbit the Sun. They are left over from when our solar system formed. They are smaller than planets and most of them live in the asteroid belt which is a region just between Mars and Jupiter, filled with hundreds of thousands of other space rocks. Asteroids can be all different shapes and sizes. Some are small, about the size of three polar bears stood on each other's shoulders, and others are pretty huge, more like the size of a 650,000 polar bear tower – wow, imagine that!

Asteroids can be made of different materials and they are split into three categories – C, S and M. C-type asteroids are carbonaceous, and the most common type of asteroid. They're tricky little things to spot because they're so dark in colour. S-type are stony asteroids and M-type are metallic. What they're made of tells us how far away from the Sun they formed. Some are exactly as they were when they first formed, whereas others have melted and then reformed, so they look a little different.

*An asteroid*

Meteor

Meteor crater

# Meteors, meteorites and meteoroids

Let's start with meteoroids shall we? These are space rocks which can range in size massively from ones as small as a greenfly to ones as big as 125 of the world's longest pythons end-to-end – eek! When these space rocks zoom through the Earth's atmosphere and burn up (sometimes even turning into super-impressive fireballs) we call them meteors. If they survive their burning road trip and land on Earth, we call them meteorites – easy-peasy really, isn't it?

If you do a little star-gazing on a clear night you might be able to see a shooting star. The name shooting star is a bit of a fib though as they aren't really stars at all! They are actually meteors and give us a beautiful natural fireworks display. Sometimes we see lots of space rocks burning up in the atmosphere at once. We call this a meteor shower and they really are something special to see.

37

# Comets

Comets are sort of like dirty cosmic snowballs. They orbit the Sun just like asteroids but when they get closer to the Sun they throw a bit of a cosmic tantrum. As they heat up, the icy bits sublimate (this is a fancy way of saying they turn straight from a solid to a gas, without becoming liquid) and that releases the gas and dust trapped within them into space. This dust and gas forms the famous comet tail shape and can be millions of kilometres long! Yikes!

Have humans ever seen a comet up close? Oh yes we have! The *Rosetta* mission was one seriously spectacular mission. This European Space Agency mission was designed to study comet 67P/Churyumov-Gerasimenko up close! The *Rosetta* spacecraft orbited the comet, had a good nose around, and a smaller spacecraft called *Philae* landed on it and probed the surface. AMAZING!

Comet Neowise seen over the pre-dawn skies of Deer Valley, Utah, in the US.

**DID YOU KNOW?** One of the most super famous comets is Halley's Comet. It's a short-period comet which is visible from Earth around once every 75 years. When can we next see Halley's Comet? Get comfy because there is still a bit of a wait, it isn't due again until 2061.

Comet ISON passing through the Virgo constellation

**Q+A: Do space rocks ever come close to Earth?** Yes, sometimes they come close(ish) to Earth, and these are called Near-Earth Objects (NEOs). Scientists keep a close eye on them so we can track what they are up to. If they get a little too close they will find themselves in the firing line — literally to be blasted off course so they don't hit us!

# Astronomers Through Time

WOWEE, there have been some interesting people in the world of astronomy and space science! Let's take a look at who some of them were and what makes them special!

**Johannes Kepler (1571–1630)**
A classic. He created three key laws of planetary motion, without which the world of astronomy would look very different today.

**Annie Maunder (1868–1947)**
Have you ever heard of solar photography? It just means photographing the Sun (safely, without burning your eyes out, of course!). Awesome Annie used solar photography to capture amazing images of the Sun's atmosphere during a total solar eclipse. Go Annie!

**William Huggins (1824–1910)**
William used a prism to split light from stars into a rainbow so he could take a closer look at their chemical make-up. What a clever-clogs!

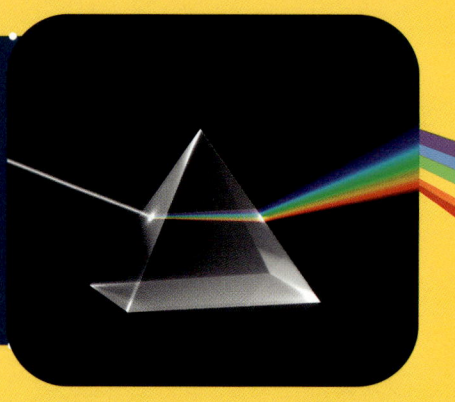

**Ahmad ibn Mājid (c.1430–1500)**
Finding your way around when you are out at sea can be a tricky business so Ahmad ibn Mājid wrote a handbook all about how to use the stars to navigate across the Indian Ocean. Not only that, he wrote the instructions as songs and poems so they would be easier to remember. Genius!

A section from 'The Book of the Benefits of the Principles and Foundations of Seamanship'

**Caroline Herschel (1750–1848)**
Caroline made some amazing discoveries in her career, particularly about comets! Who knew those dirty space snowballs could be so interesting!

**Edwin Hubble (1889–1953)**
He really is a superstar name within the world of astronomy. He realised that the Milky Way was just one of LOTS of galaxies. He also had a fluffy helper, his cat Copernicus.

**Vera Rubin (1928–2016)**
Tip Top Vera noticed that galaxies were rotating faster than they should be and that there was actually a lot more to them. She realised that because of invisible 'dark matter' they were a lot bigger than we could even see – eek!

41

**Cecilia Payne-Gaposchkin (1900–1979)**
Cecilia proposed that stars were made mainly of hydrogen and helium. At the time this was a really revolutionary idea but what do you know, she was absolutely right! High five Cecilia!

**Jocelyn Bell Burnell (b. 1943)**
Did you know stars called pulsars can rotate rapidly? No? Well no one did until Jocelyn found it out! What a cracking discovery!

**Nevil Maskelyne (1732–1811)**
Astronomers often have to work outside at night, sometimes things can get a little chilly. Nevil fixed that problem by creating an orange observing onesie! Snazzy!

**Thomas Harriot (c.1560–1621)**
Thomas was the first person known to observe the Moon through a telescope. He was a little bit reluctant to publish his work though as his patron was said to be involved in the gunpowder plot and Harriot wanted to keep his head – literally! Yikes!

42

The Lovell radio telescope

**Bernard Lovell (1913–2012)**
This resourceful astronomer used scrap pieces from old battleships to build his radio telescopes and was a real leader when it came to radio astronomy.

**Agnes Mary Clerke (1842–1907)**
Agnes was a writer who chatted to the top professional astronomers during the late-19th century to find out what they were up to, then summarised their work in popular books for everyone to read. Great stuff Agnes!

**William Herschel (1738–1822)**
He developed a bit of an obsession with making his telescopes. He used to make his own mirrors, grinding them for hours while his sister would feed him bits of food so he didn't have to take a break.

**Mary Edwards (c.1741–1815)**
Have you heard of a human computer? Well, the astounding Mary was a real whizz when it came to calculations and helped the astronomers of her time find out much more about the Moon and planets. Nice one Mary!

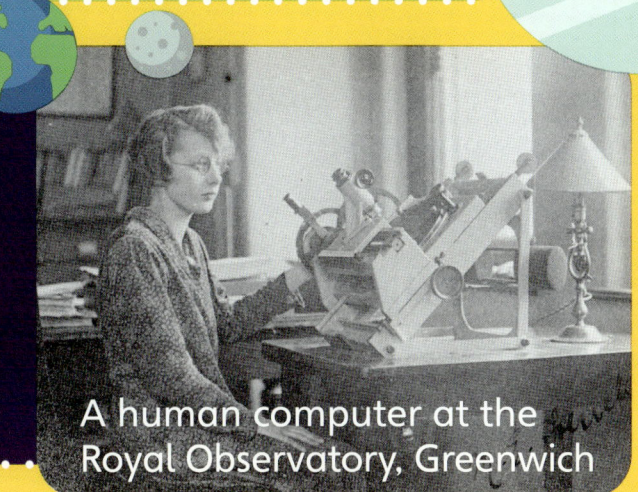

A human computer at the Royal Observatory, Greenwich

# Our Universe

Wow. What a journey. We've travelled from the very middle of our solar system to the furthest edge, and seen some amazing sights along the way. But the Solar System is actually just a teeny-tiny part of the whole Universe! So how big IS the Universe? That's an excellent question! The size of the Universe is based on a measure of all its contents, so all the planets, stars, galaxies and all the matter and energy inside. Scientists think that the Universe inflated at a seriously whizzy rate just after the Big Bang, then things calmed down and slowed a little because of the gravitational pull of new young galaxies. Since then it has been busy expanding like a huge balloon over time. We're not a little lonely planet bumbling around in space all on our own – we have interesting neighbours even if they are pretty far away. Let's take a closer look!

**FACT**
Scientists believe the Universe is 93 billion light years in diameter – now THAT is a long way!

## Stars

To start with let's chat about stars. Our wonderful Sun is the closest star and you actually have to go really, really far until you reach the next one. Proxima Centauri is the next closest star, and it's one of 100 billion stars in our galaxy. And it's 4.2 light years away. Yikes! Unfortunately you can't see it without a telescope – and the Hubble Space Telescope has taken some beautiful images of it!

**DID YOU KNOW?**
Stars sometimes look different colours. Stars that look blue are very hot, young stars whereas red ones are often cooler and getting much older. This is the opposite way to how we label taps with red and blue at home!

Betelgeuse    Rigel    Orion Nebula

**FACT**

If you want to see different colour stars all you have to do is look in the night sky at a constellation like Orion — you'll be able to see all sorts! You'll see a red star (Betelgeuse), a blue star (Rigel) and even a nebula (the Orion nebula) — a real cosmic pick 'n' mix!

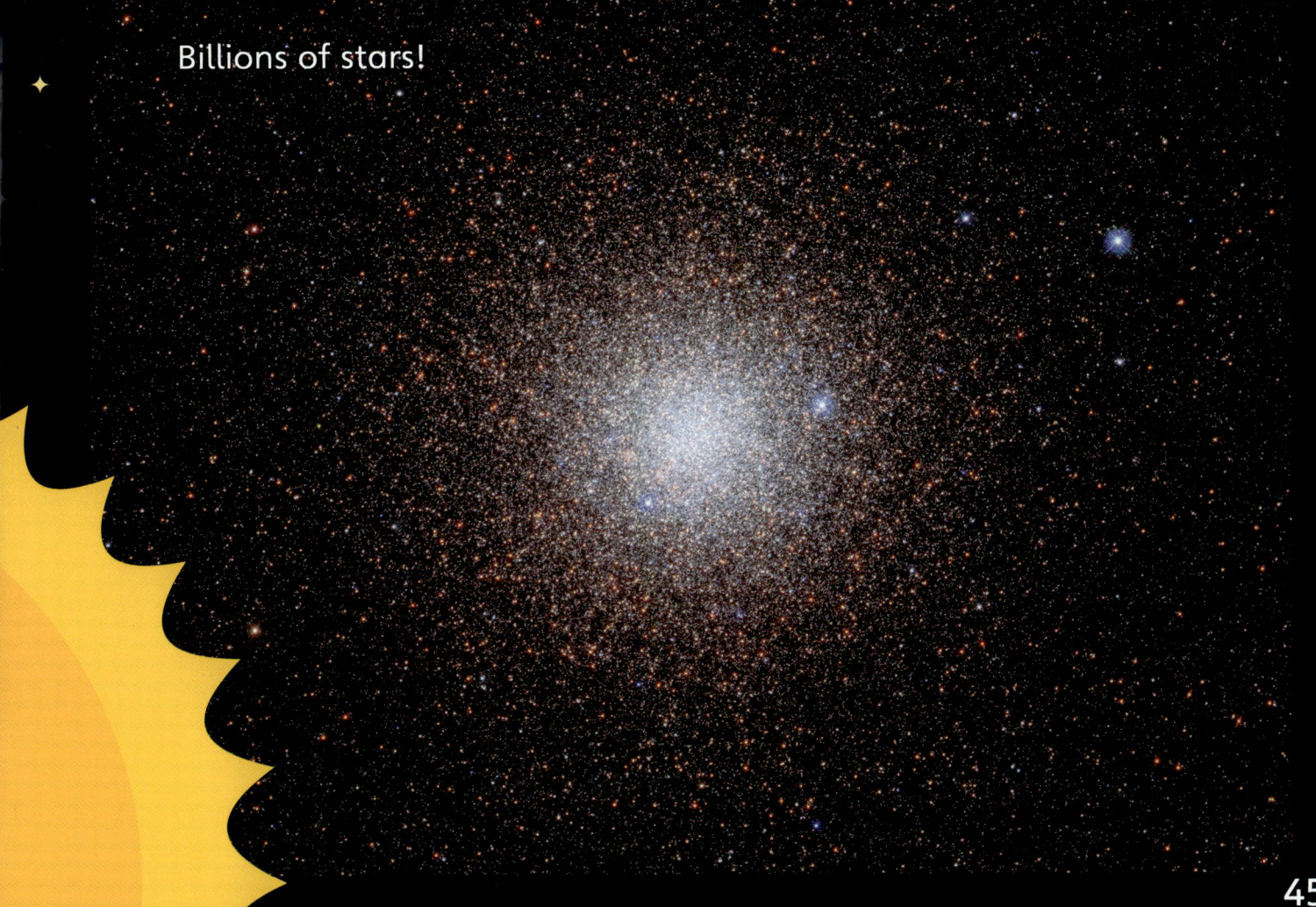

Billions of stars!

# Galaxies

The nearest galaxy to the Milky Way is called Andromeda, otherwise known as Messier 31, and it's 2.5 million light years away! Amazingly, if you have very dark and clear skies you can see this spiral galaxy yourself. It's visible with the naked eye if you look in the constellation of Andromeda, and looks a little like a fuzzy patch in the sky.

Our Universe is made of over a billion galaxies. A BILLION – that's 1,000,000,000! EEK! Our galaxy, the Milky Way, is part of what's known as the 'Local Group', which is around 30 galaxies. Andromeda is one of these and astronomers think that eventually there will be an almighty cosmic crash when it collides with our Milky Way! Don't panic though, this will be several billion years from now so we definitely don't need to worry – phew...

## DID YOU KNOW?

It takes light over 100,000 years to cross our galaxy! When we look at other galaxies their light may have taken millions or billions of light years to reach us. It's a bit like taking a photo of a flower in your garden and sending it to your friend on the other side of the world in the post. They will eventually see the picture of the flower but the real one in your garden may have wilted and died by then. Bonkers brain explosion, right?

The Andromeda Galaxy

The Whirlpool Galaxy

The Small Magellanic Cloud

Well, it's been quite the adventure travelling around our ENTIRE UNIVERSE, hasn't it?

One of the most amazing things about astronomy and space science is that there is still absolutely buckets left to learn. Maybe one day you or one of your friends can be someone who makes amazing discoveries that answer some of our biggest space science questions!

**So what are you waiting for? Get discovering!**

The Royal Observatory in Greenwich, London

### About the Author
Elizabeth Avery is an astronomer at the Royal Observatory Greenwich and a HUGE science fan! She has spent her career creating and presenting all sorts of science-based activities for people of all ages to get involved with. She has always had a serious soft spot for space science and astronomy.

### About the Royal Observatory Greenwich
The Royal Observatory, in Greenwich, London, is home to Greenwich Mean Time and the Meridian Line, and is one of the most important scientific sites in the world. Founded by Charles II in 1675, today you can explore how great scientists first mapped the seas and the stars, experience awe-inspiring astronomy and take a journey through the cosmos in London's only planetarium.